EDGE BOOKS™

✦ INTO THE GREAT OUTDOORS ✦

DEER HUNTING
For Kids

BY MATT CHANDLER

Consultant:
Greg Slone
Next Generation Hunting
Bowling Green, Kentucky

CAPSTONE PRESS
a capstone imprint

Edge Books are published by Capstone Press,
1710 Roe Crest Drive, North Mankato, Minnesota 56003.
www.capstonepub.com

Library of Congress Cataloging-in-Publication Data
Chandler, Matt.
 Deer hunting for kids / by Matt Chandler.
    p. cm.—(Edge books. into the great outdoors)
 Includes bibliographical references and index.
 Summary: "Explores the sport of deer hunting, including its rich history,
specific gear, special techniques, safety requirements, and conservation
efforts"—Provided by publisher.
 ISBN 978-1-4296-8425-5 (library binding)
 ISBN 978-1-4296-9267-0 (paperback)
 ISBN 978-1-62065-225-1 (ebook PDF)
 1. Deer hunting—Juvenile literature. I. Title.
SK301.C51146 2013
799.2'765—dc23   2011051834

Editorial Credits
Christopher L. Harbo, editor; Ted Williams, designer; Marcie Spence,
    media researcher; Sarah Schuette, photo stylist; Marcy Morin,
    scheduler; Laura Manthe, production specialist

Photo Credits
Capstone Studio: Karon Dubke, 4-5, 10, 13, 14, 22, 24-25; Dwight
R. Kuhn Photography: David Kuhn, 21, Dwight Kuhn, 16; Library
of Congress, 7; North Wind Picture Archives, 6; Shutterstock: Alfie
Photography, 8, bpk, 26, Bruce MacQueen, 1, 3, Naaman Abreu, 18,
Stephen McSweeny, 28-29, Tony Campbell, cover, 19

Printed in the United States of America in Stevens Point, Wisconsin.
032012   006678WZF12

TABLE OF CONTENTS

You're perched in a deer stand high above the ground. Suddenly a **buck** enters the clearing below you. You take aim. A bead of sweat runs down your face as you curl your finger around the trigger. You know you've only got one shot. The deer raises its head. You adjust your aim, hold your breath, and squeeze the trigger. Boom! The majestic deer staggers and falls to the ground. You climb down from your stand to inspect your deer.

buck—a male deer older than 1 year

History of Hunting

Originally deer hunting was an important part of American Indian life in North America. The meat, or venison, from a large buck could feed many members of a tribe. The bones and hide were made into tools and clothing. When Europeans arrived in the 1500s, American Indians began trading deerskins with settlers. During the height of the deerskin trade, about 5 million deer were killed each year. By the late 1800s, the whitetail deer population had dropped to about 500,000 in North America.

In the early 1900s, state and federal laws started protecting the shrinking deer population. The Lacy Act of 1900 cracked down on the trade of wild game that hunters killed illegally. The deer population soon started to rebound.

Today more than 20 million deer roam North America. Deer hunting has become a popular sport. Hunters still enjoy the venison from their deer. But the thrill of the hunt and the time spent in nature is also important. Deer hunting is a family tradition many hunters pass from generation to generation.

FACT

A deer's antlers usually grow from spring until fall. The antlers fall off in the winter, and new ones begin growing in the spring.

elk

Major Types of Deer

The types of deer most commonly hunted in North America are whitetail, elk, and mule deer. Whitetail live all across the United States, except for the Southwest, Hawaii, and Alaska. Whitetail can weigh up to 300 pounds (136 kilograms). They can run 30 miles (48 kilometers) per hour. Their name comes from the white underside of the tail they lift when alarmed.

Elk live in the mountainous western United States. They are the largest deer in North America. Elk can weigh up to 1,100 pounds (500 kg) and stand 5 feet (1.5 meters) tall.

Hunting mule deer is common in the desert areas of the western United States. Mule deer can stand up to 3.5 feet (1 m) tall. They can weigh between 130 and 280 pounds (59 and 127 kg). They get their name from their large, mulelike ears.

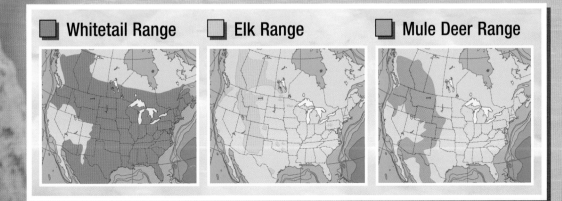

Whitetail Range   Elk Range   Mule Deer Range

CHAPTER 2

TOOLS OF THE TRADE

Without the proper equipment, it's almost impossible to bag a deer. Having a gun or bow you can handle is important. Deer stands will also help you succeed. Good hunters go into the woods with everything they need to take down a deer.

Guns and Scopes

Most people hunt deer with either a shotgun or a rifle. The most popular types of shotguns for deer hunting are the 20-gauge and the 12-gauge. For a young hunter, a 20-gauge is a good first gun. The kick, or **recoil**, when fired is less powerful than with a 12-gauge.

Depending on your state's laws, shotguns can be loaded with either buckshot shells or slug shells. Buckshot shells are packed with large pellets that spread out as they fly through the air. Slug shells fire one large bullet. Check your state's hunting laws to find out what type of shotgun ammunition is legal for hunting deer in your area.

recoil—the kickback of a gun when firing

A rifle allows a hunter to have a longer range. It fires a single bullet that can hit a target several hundred yards away. Because rifles are so powerful, some states limit their use for deer hunting.

No matter what gun you choose, adding a scope can help you take your best shot. The most common scope is a 3 x 9 scope. This means the scope **magnifies** the deer three times at its lowest reading and nine times at its highest.

Bows and Arrows

Most bowhunters use compound bows. These bows use cables and wires that allow you to easily pull back the bowstring. When choosing your bow, consider its **draw weight**. Be sure to choose a draw weight you can pull. If you can't draw your bow, you won't be ready to shoot when a deer is in sight.

magnify—to make something look larger than it really is

draw weight—a measurement of how much strength it takes to pull a bowstring back

Most bowhunters use broadhead arrows for deer hunting. These arrows can have carbon or aluminum shafts. Arrows with carbon shafts are light and fast. Arrows with aluminum shafts are heavier and can sink into the deer more deeply.

deer stand

FACT

Deer urine farms bottle and sell different types of deer urine. The best urine for attracting a buck is from a doe that is ready to mate.

Deer Stands

Many hunters use deer stands to avoid being spotted by deer. These stands get you 10 to 20 feet (3 to 6 m) above the ground. Some stands are simple platforms with seats that attach directly to tree trunks. Others include ladders and platforms that lean against and mount to trees. Some hunters even build their own free-standing deer stands.

If you buy a deer stand, consider its weight and size. Aluminum stands are lightweight and easy to set up. Choose a stand with a wide platform. A small stand doesn't give you room to move around. In cold weather your body becomes stiff and you can lose your balance. A large stand can prevent you from falling.

DEER SCENTS

Even with the best equipment, you won't bag a deer if it smells your scent. To cover their odors, some hunters use skunk scent. A drop or two of this scent makes you smell like a skunk to fool the deer. Deer are also attracted to the scent of other deer, especially during mating season. You can buy deer urine on the Internet and at specialty hunting stores. A small amount of deer urine can trick a deer into coming your way.

If you can't find a deer, all of your planning will be wasted. Scouting and tracking deer will be well worth your time. Knowing where to aim is also important if you want to be a successful hunter.

Scouting

Finding the perfect hunting spot is all about scouting before you go out to hunt. If you are unfamiliar with the area, use a field map. These maps will tell you if deer are native to the area you plan to hunt. In addition to field maps, get out and talk to people who live near the area you plan to hunt. They know the land better than anyone. Visit the places they recommend and try to find signs of deer. Then make sure your state's laws allow you to hunt in that area and ask any landowners for hunting permission. The more work you do scouting your area, the better chance you have of bagging a deer.

Tracking

Tracking deer starts on the ground. Study tracks for clues about a deer's size. For instance, a large, deep hoof print may mean a heavy buck made the track. Smaller, shallow tracks may have come from female and young deer. In addition to size, study tracks to determine how long ago the deer passed through the area. Tracks with soft round edges are probably older and worn down by rain and wind. Tracks with sharp edges tell you that a deer passed through recently. The fresher the tracks, the better your chances of spotting a deer.

FACT
Whitetail deer establish a territory and often do not stray from it. Some deer will starve to death rather than leave their established territory.

Tracking deer also involves antler rubs. To mark his territory, a buck rubs his antlers in a pattern on trees. Doing so alerts other bucks to stay away while he is trying to find a doe to mate with. As you walk through the woods, look for places where bark has been rubbed off the tree. These rubs are usually 2 to 4 feet (0.6 to 1.2 m) off the ground. If you see a pattern of rubs on several trees in the area, you know a buck is marking his territory.

Where to Aim

You have a clear shot at a large buck 50 yards (45 m) away. But where do you aim your gun? For most hunters, a shot to the deer's lungs gives them the best chance at a quick kill. The lungs of an adult buck are the size of a football. If you are a great **marksman**, you can shoot for the heart. It's a small target, but it will guarantee a fast kill.

Bowhunters have to make adjustments to where they aim. An arrow is much slower than a bullet. Sometimes deer can hear the snap of your bowstring. The sound can startle the deer, causing it to lower its body slightly before springing forward. This split second movement, called string jumping, can make your arrow miss its target. To avoid missing your mark, aim a little lower than the heart and lungs. If the deer moves, your arrow should still strike it. If the deer stays still, you also have a strike.

marksman—a person skilled at aiming and shooting guns

FIELD DRESSING

After you've shot your deer, it's time for field dressing. Field dressing is important because bleeding inside the deer's carcass can spoil the meat. Properly field dressing your deer can save the venison.

To field dress a deer, you'll need a knife and a game saw to remove the organs. Also make sure you have disposable gloves to protect your hands, a cloth for clean-up, and plastic bags for the organs.

targeting the lungs

FACT

A wounded deer that doesn't die right away leaks hormones that can make the meat taste bad. A quick "kill shot" can improve the flavor of the meat.

CHAPTER 4

SAFETY FIRST

FACT

Deer are color-blind. To them, blaze orange looks brown and blends in with the woods.

Deer hunting is an exciting sport, but it does include some risks. It's important to follow a few safety rules in the field as you hunt.

General Safety

No matter what you hunt, some basic safety precautions should be followed every time. Before you set out, tell someone where and how long you will be out. Also pack a basic survival kit. Include a cell phone, water, rope, first-aid supplies, a knife, and a waterproof fire-starting kit.

Blaze Orange

Imagine being perched in your tree stand. You see something big move in the brush below you. You take aim. Are you positive it is a deer? From a distance it can be hard to tell the difference between a deer and a hunter. That's why most states require firearm hunters to wear blaze orange vests or jackets over their clothes. Blaze orange is easy for other hunters to see. Bowhunters are usually not required to wear blaze orange unless they hunt during firearm season.

Deer Stand Safety

Staying safe while climbing and sitting in your stand is very important. Never try to carry your gun or bow and arrows up into your deer stand with you. Instead, tie a rope around your unloaded weapon and leave it on the ground. Once you have safely climbed into your stand, raise your weapon up to you with the rope. Also be sure to wear a safety harness while sitting in your stand. A harness will keep you from falling if you lose your balance.

Gun and Bow Safety

A big part of weapons safety is being aware of your surroundings. Pay attention to who and what is around you and keep your gun pointed in a safe direction. Always keep your gun's **safety** on until you are ready to fire. If you are hunting with a bow, keep your arrows in a **quiver** until you are ready to use them. The quiver will protect you from the razor-sharp arrowheads if you trip and fall.

> **safety**—a device that prevents a gun from firing

> **quiver**—a container for arrows

For many people, deer hunting is a tradition they look forward to every year. But keeping that tradition alive requires the work of **conservation** groups and responsible hunters.

Conservation Groups

Conservation groups play an important part in supporting the deer hunting tradition. Whitetails Unlimited is an organization that focuses on whitetail deer. Founded in 1982, Whitetails Unlimited raises money for hunting education, deer **habitat** protection, and wildlife research.

In 1984 the Rocky Mountain Elk Foundation began its work to improve and protect North American elk habitats. Since it formed, the organization has helped restore elk populations in the United States and Canada.

conservation—the protection of animals and plants, as well as the wise use of what we get from nature

habitat—the natural place and conditions in which an animal or plant lives

Responsible Hunting

Being a responsible hunter is the best way to protect deer populations. Always leave your hunting area in its natural condition. Deer often avoid areas where hunters have left things behind. Pick up spent shell casings and other litter. Avoid damaging the natural environment by cutting and clearing brush.

Being a responsible hunter also means obeying laws and limits. Most states divide the hunting season into firearms season and bow season. The laws also limit how many and what type of deer can be taken. These rules prevent hunters from thinning the population too much.

As a deer hunter, your role in the sport keeps the tradition going strong. Remember that careful preparation and patience are the keys to success. As you watch a buck walk into the clearing ahead of you, you'll feel the thrill of the hunt. And when you take aim and shoot, you'll know your hard work paid off.

GLOSSARY

buck (BUHK)—a male deer older than 1 year

conservation (kon-sur-VAY-shuhn)—the protection of animals and plants, as well as the wise use of what we get from nature

draw weight (DRAW WATE)—a measurement of how much strength it takes to pull a bowstring back

habitat (HAB-uh-tat)—the natural place and conditions in which an animal or plant lives

magnify (MAG-nih-fye)—to make something look larger than it really is

marksman (MARKS-muhn)—a person skilled at aiming and shooting guns

quiver (KWIV-ur)—a container for arrows

range (RAYNJ)—the longest distance at which a weapon can still hit its target

recoil (RI-koil)—the kickback of a gun when firing

safety (SAYF-tee)—a device that prevents a gun from firing

READ MORE

Adamson, Thomas K. *Deer Hunting*. Wild Outdoors. Mankato, Minn.: Capstone Press, 2011.

DiLorenzo, Michael. *Bows, Does & Bucks!: An Introduction to Archery Deer Hunting*. Clinton Township, Mich.: Running Moose Publications, Inc., 2010.

MacRae, Sloan. *Deer Hunting*. Open Season. New York: PowerKids Press, 2011.

INTERNET SITES

FactHound offers a safe, fun way to find Internet sites related to this book. All of the sites on FactHound have been researched by our staff.

Here's all you do:

Visit *www.facthound.com*

Type in this code: 9781429684255

Check out projects, games and lots more at
www.capstonekids.com

INDEX